Bar and Bat Mitzvahs

Robert
Walker

Crabtree Publishing Company

www.crabtreebooks.com

Crabtree Publishing Company

www.crabtreebooks.com

Author: Robert Walker

Editorial director: Kathy Middleton

Editor: Crystal Sikkens

Photo research: Margaret Amy Salter, Crystal Sikkens

Design: Ken Wright

Cover design: Margaret Amy Salter

Print coordinator: Katherine Berti

Production coordinator: Ken Wright

Prepress technician: Ken Wright

Photographs:
Alamy: Miriam Reik: page 1; Imagestate Media
Partners Limited Impact Photos: page 15
Fotolia: Graham Photography: cover (right), pages 5,
31; Alan: page 26
iStockphoto: page 14
Keystone Press: Mark Richards/KPA-ZUMA: page 29
Library of Congress: page 30
Shutterstock: cover (left), pages 4, 9, 12, 13, 16, 22;
Maksim Dubinsky: page 18; Stavchansky Yakov:
page 19; Rob Swanson: page 20
Thinkstock: pages 6, 7, 10, 11, 21, 24, 25
Wikimedia Commons: Steve Petteway, Collection of
the Supreme Court of the United States: page 8;
EdoM: page 17; Berthold Werner: page 23; Tatiana
Sapateiro: page 27; Selena N.B.H: page 28

Library and Archives Canada Cataloguing in Publication

Walker, Robert, 1980-
    Bar and bat mitzvahs / Robert Walker.

(Celebrations in my world)
Includes index.
Issued also in electronic format.
ISBN 978-0-7787-4086-5 (bound).--ISBN 978-0-7787-4091-9 (pbk.)

    1. Bar mitzvah--Juvenile literature. 2. Bat mitzvah--Juvenile
literature. 3. Jewish way of life--Juvenile literature. I. Title.
II. Series: Celebrations in my world

BM707.W35 2012   j296.4'424   C2012-900900-8

Library of Congress Cataloging-in-Publication Data

Walker, Robert.
Bar and bat mitzvahs / Robert Walker.
p. cm. -- (Celebrations in my world)
Includes index.
ISBN 978-0-7787-4086-5 (reinforced library binding : alk. paper) -- ISBN 978-0-
7787-4091-9 (pbk. : alk. paper) -- ISBN 978-1-4271-7845-9 (electronic pdf) --
ISBN 978-1-4271-7960-9 (electronic html)
1. Bar-mitzvah--Juvenile literature. 2. Bat-mitzvah--Juvenile literature. I. Title.

BM707.W35 2012
296.4'424--dc23

2012004070

Crabtree Publishing Company

www.crabtreebooks.com   1-800-387-7650

Printed in the U.S.A./052012/FA20120413

Published in Canada
Crabtree Publishing
616 Welland Ave.
St. Catharines, Ontario
L2M 5V6

Published in the United States
Crabtree Publishing
PMB 59051
350 Fifth Avenue, 59th Floor
New York, New York 10118

Published in the United Kingdom
Crabtree Publishing
Maritime House
Basin Road North, Hove
BN41 1WR

Published in Australia
Crabtree Publishing
3 Charles Street
Coburg North
VIC 3058

Contents

What is a Bar Mitzvah/ Bat Mitzvah?

A Bar Mitzvah and a Bat Mitzvah are coming of age ceremonies for young boys and girls of the Jewish religion. It marks the age when a child is considered to have become a young adult.

- A Bar Mitzvah or Bat Mitzvah takes place in a **synagogue**, or Jewish place of worship.

DID YOU KNOW?

In the Jewish faith, the age of adulthood for a boy is 13 years old, and 12 for a girl.

Bar Mitzvah and Bat Mitzvah are not only the names of the ceremonies, they are also the titles that the young people are given. *Bar Mitzvah* is Hebrew for "son of the **commandment**," and *Bat Mitzvah* means "daughter of the commandment." This means the youths are now officially a part of the Jewish community.

As part of a Bar Mitzvah or Bat Mitzvah, the young person must carry the **Torah**, or holy text of the Jewish faith, around the synagogue.

5

An Important Day

After a young person's Bar Mitzvah or Bat Mitzvah, he or she is now responsible for obeying the rules, or commandments, of the Jewish faith. According to the Jewish faith, he or she can now tell the difference between right and wrong and are **accountable** for what they do.

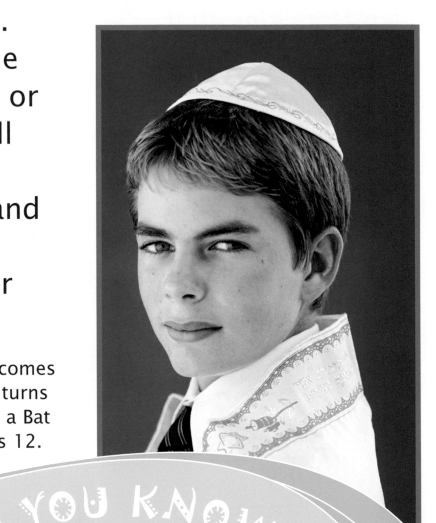

- A boy automatically becomes a Bar Mitzvah when he turns 13, and a girl becomes a Bat Mitzvah when she turns 12.

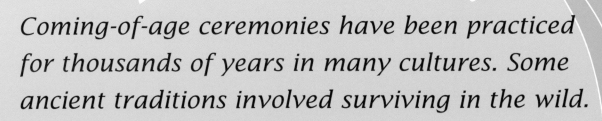

DID YOU KNOW?

Coming-of-age ceremonies have been practiced for thousands of years in many cultures. Some ancient traditions involved surviving in the wild.

After a Bar Mitzvah or Bat Mitzvah, the young person is also expected to increase their involvement in Jewish religious practices. This includes **fasting** during Yom Kippur, one of the most important events in the Jewish religious calendar. Young men and women are also encouraged to volunteer as tutors for other youths waiting to take their own Bar Mitzvah or Bat Mitzvah.

Family plays an important part in a Bar Mitzvah or Bat Mitzvah. They offer support and help the young person prepare for the big day.

7

Judaism

Judaism is one of the world's oldest religions. It is believed to have begun in present day Israel almost 4,000 years ago. Today, Judaism is practiced around the globe. Some of history's greatest writers, scientists, and businesspeople have been of the Jewish faith.

● Ruth Bader Ginsburg is the first Jewish woman ever appointed to the Supreme Court of the United States.

DID YOU KNOW?

Israelites is an ancient name for Jewish people. This was the name given to the people who lived in the ancient kingdom of Israel.

Hebrew was originally the language spoken by Jewish people. Jewish biblical text and prayers are written in Hebrew. According to Jewish beliefs, everything in life is controlled by a single God. It is believed that God gave a set of rules called the Ten Commandments to the Jewish prophet Moses. These rules are what followers of God are supposed to live by.

Other Christian religions also follow the Ten Commandments. Many synagogues and churches have paintings that show Moses holding the stone tablets that contained the Ten Commandments.

9

The Sabbath

The Sabbath is the seventh day of the Jewish week. It begins Friday evening and ends Saturday evening. Resting on the Sabbath is one of the Ten Commandments. It is believed that God created the Heavens and Earth in six days and rested on the seventh. Therefore Jews who observe the Sabbath will not do any work on this day.

● The Sabbath begins with the lighting of candles and a prayer.

Originally the Sabbath was intended for prayer and Torah study. Today, most Jewish families use it as a time to get together and enjoy each others company. But they still follow the "no work" rule, and hurry to have any cooking and other preparations done before Friday evening.

Celebrating the Sabbath allows Jews to rest, recite blessings, and spend time with family.

Girls Get Their Own Day

Bat Mitzvahs are a relatively new practice in the Jewish faith. For many years there was no ceremony to mark when a young woman entered into adulthood. **Rabbi** Mordecai Kaplan believed men and women should be treated as equals, so, in 1922, he held the first Bat Mitzvah for his daughter, Judith.

During a Bat Mitzvah, the young girl reads from the Torah.

DID YOU KNOW?

The page numbers in this book are shown inside an important Jewish symbol. The Star of David is a six-pointed star made from two triangles.

A Bat Chayil is usually held on a Sunday, and includes singing and a short speech by the young woman.

Instead of a Bat Mitzvah, some Jewish groups will hold a ceremony called a Bat Chayil, which means "daughter of excellence," when a girl reaches age 12. Young women will study the laws of the Sabbath and other important practices. Unlike a Bat Mitzvah, the girl doesn't read from the Torah during a Bat Chayil.

Important Religious Texts

The Torah is the first five holy books of the Jewish scriptures, or sacred writings. The Torah tells stories about the creation of the universe, the lives of Jewish prophets, and different mitzvoths, or commandments, of the Jewish faith.

- The Torah is written from right to left. Often, people use a pointer called a yad to help read it.

DID YOU KNOW?

The five books in the Torah are named Genesis, Exodus, Leviticus, Numbers, and Deuteronomy.

The Torah is the most important religious text for a Bar Mitzvah and Bat Mitzvah. Most of the young person's reading will be done from the Torah. There is also the Talmud, which contains Jewish civil, or public, and ceremonial laws. The Talmud helps Jewish people understand the Torah and how its teachings can be put into practice in daily life.

● The Torah scrolls are kept in a special cupboard called the Aron Hakodesh, or the Ark.

17

At the Synagogue

The synagogue is the most important place of worship for Jews. Its design, both inside and out, ranges from simple to elaborate. All synagogues, however, have an Ark that holds the Torah and other important religious writings. The Ark is the main feature of the synagogue and is often beautifully decorated.

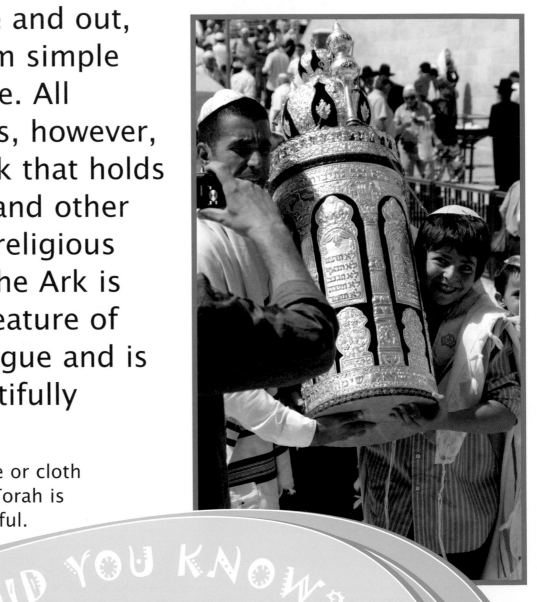

● The wooden case or cloth covering of the Torah is also quite beautiful.

DID YOU KNOW?

A synagogue is also called a house of study and a house of prayer.

Synagogues are also called temples in honor of the ancient Temple Mount in Jerusalem. The Temple Mount was once the center of the whole Jewish faith. All that remains of the temple is the Western Wall, and it is the most holy site in Judaism. It is a huge **open-air** synagogue, receiving many visitors everyday, both Jewish and other faiths.

● Some people will insert written prayers into the gaps between the stones of the Western Wall.

The Hebrew Language

Hebrew is one of the oldest languages in human history. The earliest examples of the Hebrew alphabet can be traced all the way back to 1000 B.C. Today, there are two versions of Hebrew, classical and modern. Classical Hebrew is used by Jews for prayer and study. Modern Hebrew is the official language spoken in Israel.

שער שכם
باب العامود
Damascus Gate

הר הצופים
هار هتسوفيم
Mt Scopus

מעלה אדומים
معلي ادوميم
Ma'ale Adumim

Signs in Israel are written in modern Hebrew.

DID YOU KNOW?

Around 70 A.D., Hebrew fell out of popular use and was only used in Jewish worship. Around 1880, Eliezer ben Yehuda revived the language creating modern Hebrew.

When written, Hebrew runs from right to left on the page. The Hebrew alphabet has 22 letters and no vowels. Unlike English, there are no capital letters. None of the letters touch, and all the words are separated by a space.

Learning to read and speak Hebrew can be very difficult for someone who is not familiar with it.

21

Getting Prepared

Jewish children prepare for their Bat Mitzvah or Bar Mitzvah by going to a special school called a **cheder**. Here, they get a better understanding about the Torah and its teachings. Often, boys and girls will study for several years to prepare for the Bar Mitzvah and Bat Mitzvah.

Many Jewish children are also taught to read and write Hebrew at cheders.

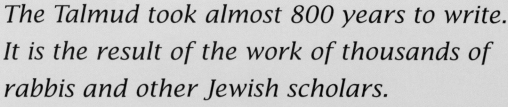

DID YOU KNOW?

The Talmud took almost 800 years to write. It is the result of the work of thousands of rabbis and other Jewish scholars.

22

As the day approaches, Jewish boys and girls meet with a tutor as well as with their rabbi who will be overseeing the event. The parents of the Bar Mitzvah and Bat Mitzvah invite family and friends to attend the celebration. They also organize the reception afterward.

● This poster is advertising a Bar Mitzvah. The family is inviting the public to come and witness the ceremony.

The Big Day

On the day of his or her Bar Mitzvah or Bat Mitzvah the young person often wears a prayer shawl called a tallit. This is a sign that he or she has become an adult. During the ceremony, the Bar Mitzvah or Bat Mitzvah will read selected passages from the Torah. They will also carry the Torah around the synagogue.

- Some Bar Mitzvahs also wear **tefillin** which are two small boxes containing parts of the Torah. One is strapped to his head and the other to his arm.

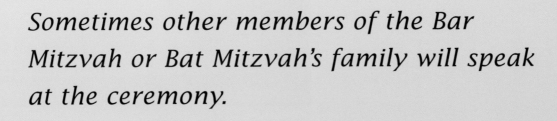

DID YOU KNOW?

Sometimes other members of the Bar Mitzvah or Bat Mitzvah's family will speak at the ceremony.

24

It is customary for the father of the child to recite what is called the **baruch shepatarani**. This is a prayer to God offering thanks for the gift of children. It also officially announces that the parents are no longer accountable for their child's actions.

The rabbi then offers his congratulations to the young person, and the service comes to an end.

● On the Sabbath, wine and bread called challah are eaten. During a Bar Mitzvah or Bat Mitzvah, the young person delivers the blessing over these items.

25

The Reception

The Bar Mitzvah or Bat Mitzvah ceremony is usually followed by a reception afterward. Family and friends join the Bar Mitzvah or Bat Mitzvah for dinner, dancing, and entertainment. It is an opportunity for family and friends to congratulate the young person and spend some quality time together.

- The reception hall is often decorated to look much like a wedding reception.

DID YOU KNOW?

A boy or girl will only be allowed to complete their Bar Mitzvah or Bat Mitzvah if their rabbi feels they are prepared.

At the reception, the Bar Mitzvah or Bat Mitzvah gives a short speech called a **derasha** where they thank their parents, family, and rabbi. The young person may also light candles in honor of their family members and explain how they have affected their life so far. The meal, known as the seudat mitzvah, is normally served with foods that are **kosher**. Kosher means the food was prepared according to certain Jewish rules.

● The Bar Mitzvah or Bat Mitzvah often receives a cake and gifts from his or her guests.

27

Let's Party!

After the dinner and speeches are finished, the reception moves on to the dancing and entertainment. Many receptions today include both modern and traditional Jewish music and songs. Some families may hire live entertainment, such as a band or a magician, to entertain their guests.

Some families give out party favors to their guests. These can include cookies, candies, or even hats and accessories.

DID YOU KNOW?

Years ago, a boy becoming a Bar Mitzvah would have a poem published in his honor.

A traditional dance often included at a Bar Mitzvah or Bat Mitzvah reception is the Hora dance. For this dance, guests join hands in a large circle. They move together to the right, criss-crossing and kicking up their feet. The Bat Mitzvah or Bar Mitzvah is often lifted up on a chair in the middle of the circle.

The parents and other family members get their turn on the chair after the Bar Mitzvah or Bat Mitzvah.

29

Then and Now

Hundreds of years ago, a Bar Mitzvah was a small, modest celebration. The food was simple, the service was short, and the number of guests was small. Many Bar Mitzvahs were held on the same day as major Jewish holidays in the hope of having more people able to attend.

● Early Bar Mitzvahs simply marked the occasion of a boy's first reading of the Torah after his 13th birthday.

DID YOU KNOW?

Bar Mitzvahs have been celebrated since the 14th century in the late Middle Ages.

Today, especially in North America, Bar Mitzvahs and Bat Mitzvahs have become very big deals. The reception, in particular, has become larger and more elaborate over the years. Many families celebrate a Bar Mitzvah or Bat Mitzvah with as much **extravagance** as other major life events, such as a prom or wedding.

● Regardless of how elaborate the receptions have become, the importance of becoming a Bar Mitzvah or Bat Mitzvah has not changed.

31

Glossary

accountable Responsible for their actions or decisions

baruch shepatarani A father's blessing at a Bar Mitzvah

cheder A Jewish place of learning

commandment A rule from God

derasha A Jewish sermon

extravagance A large expensive event or item

fasting Not eating.

kosher Food prepared according to Jewish rules

open air A space open to the outdoors

rabbi A Jewish teacher

Sabbath The Jewish day of rest

synagogue A Jewish place of worship

tefillin Small boxes containing Jewish text

tradition The passing down of customs or beliefs

Index